Black Swan Speaks

PICKING UP THE PIECES AND
EMBRACING MY TREASURE

ROMY FLORENCE

PAGE PUBLISHING
Conneaut Lake, PA

First originally published by Page Publishing 2022

ISBN 978-1-6624-8472-8 (pbk)
ISBN 978-1-6624-8473-5 (digital)

Printed in the United States of America

This anthology is dedicated to the memory of my late grandparents, father, and husband:

Evelyn Estelle (Schenck) Lovett
William Julius Lovett Sr.
Lillie Ruth (Rackley) Florence
Ernest Florence
Wallace Florence
Scott William Walker

To the lives they lived, full of strength, wisdom, and courage. The fights they fought, pain they endured, and the fulfillment of their lives. May their examples and lessons taught always be remembered.

Contents

◇◇◇

Foreword

◇◇◇◇◇◇◇◇◇◇◇◇◇◇◇◇◇◇◇◇◇◇◇◇◇◇◇◇◇◇◇◇◇

Telling a story, compiling your thoughts and feelings is not an easy task. Getting a message out to people that is close to the heart is sometimes misunderstood. Everyone has a story to tell. My thoughts describe how I overcame what I considered nightmares in my life. From a family with unknown abandonment issues, to broken marriages, to financial woes, to a new beginning is the path I have traveled. Never closing an eye to the past, but continuously looking forward to the bright sunshine ahead. There's always a starting point, and you won't reach the end until you are ready. I wasn't ready. I had to keep moving through my many storms until I realized that life is meaningful and the love I desire is *real*. So I had to *pick up the pieces.*

This writing is an affirmation of how I reclaimed myself. With all the best intentions, the compilation of many thoughts and ideas that relate directly to the relationships I found myself in could've been detrimental to my psyche. Having been taught how to work out problems, I was confronted with life decisions that had to be made by me and me alone. I had to step up and make *real* decisions about *real* life issues despite what others thought. I must say, you should never talk about your situation to a lot of people. Their baggage may cloud your judgment. Most situations may be similar in nature, but they are not the same. Through my writing, I believe I can help someone else understand that they too, are more than a *survivor*. The circumstances, trials, obstacles, and challenges open your eyes to a world that you may sometimes feel is only occupied by you. It did not matter whether I was happy or sad; I just wrote my thoughts and feelings down so I could remember these moments in time. This was my therapy without seeing a doctor; this is how I soothed myself; this was my period of meditation and soul-searching to find out just how I would deal with *my* dilemmas. I made a decision – the right one! Here I am today, publicly speaking about it!

Along the way, I lost loved ones, but their memories are very much a part of me and alive in my heart. My love pours out to my mother and sister who are in my corner no matter what, my daughters who have been my underlying source of strength and support – my rocks in a weary land. The look in their innocent eyes and the life we built together is what I live for. We did it together, and I can finally *embrace my treasure!*

I'm Me

◇◇◇

I find solace in writing because it expresses my freedom
The ability to "just be" is liberating without condition
I think about my varied talents and accomplishments
     and cannot identify ONE
that takes the lead
What I can say is that they are all-encompassing and
     together they make me who I
am – I love me; I'm impressed by me and I like me!
There's nothing I would change about me
I am my own best friend and when I converse with
     the little girl in me, I am at awe
with what I see, hear, and do.
She has her own ideas and I allow her to launch her
     platforms within – in me!
I am authentically true to myself and that's all that
     matters.
Can you relate?

Hello

◇◇◇

The early morning sounds of birds chirping give way
    to a new day.
The quiet allows you to think and reflect about what's
    on the horizon and how it
impacts your happy place.
Your mind explores the ebbs and flows of unchar-
    tered territory.
You are clear like an untouched canvas awaiting the
    design of an artist's stroke!

These Old Knees

◇◇◇◇◇◇◇◇◇◇◇◇◇◇◇◇◇◇◇◇◇◇◇◇◇◇◇◇◇◇◇◇◇◇◇◇

These Old Knees, why you treat me so bad,
We go way back to some of the best times ever had.
From the beginning, you had me on lock and all my
       tumbling contributed to your *tick tock.*
Time flew when we were having fun,
I had no idea your days would be numbered, and you
       would tell me *"I'm done!"*
I didn't take you for granted; for you elevated me in
       more ways than I was slanted.
Running, tumbling, walking and just being you were.
Until that dreadful day that brought about a stir.
You've been telling me for some time now
That you're waving a white flag
And I must make a decision that will make me sad.
These Old Knees have seen their *last days,*
My memories hold all of the replays.
As I say goodbye and welcome your successors,
I can rid my body of all distresses.
New adventures I anticipate with a smile
Because I have been in pain for a while.
I love you but will love them more
For my new beginnings await new things to explore.

These Old Knees, These Old Knees
I will again sleep at night with comfort and ease.

Bionic Woman

◇◇◇

Here we go again! On a trip
To revive my lost dip because of my hip.
Was it really in the cards for me to be
so selfishly wearing you down until all I was wearing
was a frown?
I apologize for the years of missteps
and unexpected jars that caused you to freak out; we
have reached *"that point"*
and "ole girl" has to come out! No more waiting and
putting off until the next time;
your home is getting upgraded to
"PRIME TIME."
Half of me is on the bionic tip and you know what
happens when the stars *"Shine"*
Elektra makes her appealing appearance like *fine wine.*
She's preparing to meander through the medical
environment with style and grace
at a pace fit for a **Goddess** – steady, no rush, no race.
I'm getting ready to receive my new baby. I'm going
to take care of her so that
she allows me to flourish making my quality of life
free from pain and angst.

I'm getting back on my grind with the wind racing
    past my ear celebrating the
new and improved "Elektra, The Bionic Woman!"
IT'S MY WORLD!

I'm in Love

◇◇◇

I'm in love and I know it's true
You're on my mind every waking moment—
The missing piece I've longed for that puts me at ease.
Your words are ever so calming.
I am marrying for the third time, and this is the *only*
     husband I've ever had!

Cleave

◇◇◇◇◇◇◇◇◇◇◇◇◇◇◇◇◇◇◇◇◇◇◇◇◇◇◇◇◇◇◇◇◇◇◇◇

You get me
I get you
Whether in mixed company or in
a public forum, you support me.
As I cleave unto you, I share my most intimate thoughts
    and secrets. I navigate every encounter with you
only to find myself yearning to be forever by your side.
Is this a whirlwind affair or is it what I've been look-
    ing for?
My heart says two who can share, understand.
It's a love language that is cultivated with time.
With time being your friend, there's always room in
    the Inn.
We get each other!

That's Him

<><><><><><><><><><><><><><><><><><><><><><><><><><><>

Your masculinity screams Confidence and Strength!
Your swag is on 1000!
We have a genuine connection other than physical
    and vibe understanding each other without
    clouding our judgment
by moving too quickly with sex.
Slow and steady wins the race. There's no need to worry
when you're around. Your presence sends shock
    waves through the air announcing you are my
    man and proud of it.
You worry about nothing but have my back in all I do.
The consistency and attention pull at my heartstrings
    because
you never disappoint. Are you seeking the treasure?
Perhaps you want to polish a diamond in the rough?
Either way, the selfless interaction you display creates
    an emotional cloud that is transparent.
I can see clearly now, you are that dude!

You Up on My Neck

◇◇

You up on my neck
I like you there.
Sniffing, licking, and kissing.
Searching for the key that ignites the fire.
The ever-flowing passion signals
The ways we share remind us that our
Connectivity is more exciting than ultraviolet light.
You up on my neck
I like you there.
exposing the realness of a true love
some only see in dreams. We're raw and
sensitive; enjoying the pleasures that only we
can create but always acknowledging the
fragrance of the day.

I'm Speaking

Each day there reflects a moment. What you derive
from the events of the past, even if it were
yesterday, gives you the ability to choose how to nav-
igate your growth.
Some things we know, some things we don't, and if
we're lucky, we'll discover new ideas and imple-
ment them. My voice is loud and real.
I'm no longer held captive inside myself screaming
to get out.
Can you hear me?

Girl Power

◇◇

Girls, we are on our way. Tight as tight can be.
Singing, laughing, and riding in our van so everyone
    can see.
Girls, we are on our way!

Sistas

◇◇

As we navigated through the pandemic over the past
    year,
it was extra-special figuring out how we'd keep in touch.
With the country on lockdown, nowhere to go and
    the loss
of in-person gatherings, we made it happen!
Technology took hold of us and enabled awesome
    fellowships via Zoom. We celebrated birthdays
    monthly with a DJ
and invited guests. It was the only way we could see
    each other
and laugh together. A delightful suggestion was made
    for us
to have a photo shoot. As we pondered what we
    would wear,
T-shirts and some form of denim bottom was approved.
We also decided to wear fedora hats and sandals.
Excitement was in the air! The fedoras came in too many
colors to name and the selection process began.
We even booked a reservation at a steak house for dinner
afterwards. It was such a beautiful experience.
People asked us what we were celebrating

and the answer was "The Love of Sisterhood!"
This group of women boast over forty years of
friendship. Getting together to celebrate drive-by
birthdays,
Superbowl Sundays, Comedy Club Nights and
a home movie theatre with a concession stand were
highlights of our pandemic engagement. Showing love
and supporting one another in all we do
collectively and individually. Capturing this moment
in time
was our Photographer Extraordinaire, Mr. Brandon
Brown.
It was important for us to embrace what we look like
through his lenses. We met at an upscale garden venue
where we were greeted and met with mimosas.
The floral décor was breathtaking and complimented
our swag.

A Lady

<><><><><><><><><><><><><><><><><><><><><><><><><><><><><>

I put my favorite perfume in my lowest crevice and
    dare you to go down there and sniff it!
My aroma mesmerizes men and forces them to fol-
    low my scent.
I'm hands-off and ONLY for show.
I'd like to think it was the latter.
Meaningful conversations have evolved from our ini-
    tial dialogue. I'm a Lady and you treat me as
    such with high regard for my feelings. I like that!
Nothing is one-sided and we complement each other
    with lifetime enhancements. The curve of it all
    rests with the Union of a King and Queen. Our
    reign is destined to reach heights unseen. It is
    within our reach,
So, Let's SOAR!

You Can Make It

<><><><><><><><><><><><><><><><><><><><><><><><><><><><><><><><>

You can make it
If you believe in what you do
You can make it
With support on demand
You can see things through
With your faith it's true
Just one step at a time
You'll make it to the other side
Waste not, want not
You can make it

Oh, So Funny

◇◇◇

You are some character
You make me laugh
You make me cry and sigh.
Oh, how I like your humor, your style, your hook!
Keep the people laughing, it's very healthy and does
a body good!

Love, Laughter, and Happily Ever After

◇◇

From the moment we officially met and began to
 openly share, I felt an immediate attraction
to your heart and soul. You embraced all of me and
 made me feel
the safest I've ever felt in my life. Nothing else mattered.
You captured my mind and engaged me so that all I
 could do was
Clutch my pearls and go with the flow – and I must say,
A never-ending flow!
You acknowledge the past that keeps us current.
 Today I marry my best friend, my
Lover, my protector, and the man who holds the key
 to my dreams. As I reflect on life lived thus far;
 I'm amazed at how we have been on the same
 page since day one and have continued to
affirm each other with authenticity. You have encour-
 aged me to speak
my truth and to never feel like I cannot express myself.

You get me; you listen to my heart; you take the time
        to hear me to respond accordingly.
We have so much room for things to get
better and better as each day passes.
This is our Tribe: We have no place to go but up.
I proclaim to all that I love you with my entire being.
I've never felt more certain about anything in my life,
and spending it with you is what I am destined to do.
You are my King!

Learning to Forgive

◇◇

Forgiveness is a personal journey. It's something that
    you internalize because it can be consuming.
Being able to humble oneself to put aside what you
    consider
Wrongdoing is no easy task.
People are afraid to address their inner turmoil when
    they have been betrayed.
The circumstances may or may not be true.
The situation may not be
worthy of self-inflicted pain. People do not realize it
    creates a disturbance
throughout the body.
Learning to forgive relieves the stress, frees your mind
    of unnecessary thoughts,
and allows one to be at peace with accepting choices
    others make. You will encounter things and
    relationships
That are problematic and you can find it within
    yourself to
pick and choose your battles. I'm not saying you have
    to forget but
in time, the thought will fade away.

In order to move forward, we must weigh our options
        and identify the things most important to us. Is
        it worth carrying
a torch for something that will wear on us
creating an ilk inside that tears us apart? Can we for-
        give others of transgressions,
and permit ourselves to continue to live, love, and
        laugh together? I'm sure the
latter is the preferred move.

Exhale

◇◇

Take a deep breath
Let it go
Take another
Let it go too!
Think about one of your proudest moments and
Take another breath
Let it go slowly and sigh,
"Exhale, Exhale, Exhale!"

The Black Jelly Bean

<><><><><><><><><><><><><><><><><><><><><><><><><><><><>

With all of the colors in the bag, why do so many people dislike the black jelly bean? As a child, I was never a fan of it. People, including myself, would take every other color except the black one. I've heard it tasted nasty and lacked the fruitiness of the others.

As the years have passed, I felt the black jelly bean needed an advocate. This jelly bean was singled out, frowned upon, ridiculed, discarded, and isolated. It felt real and related to what we have come to know as "colorism."

What you don't know is that the black jellybean tastes like "Sambuca" – an Italian anise-flavored, colorless liqueur. It is a special jelly bean that has purpose by design. The taste is debatable, but I prefer the sambuca taste. The black jelly bean is regal with a rich history. There has never been an acceptable reason given for the disdain the black jellybean has encountered.

Suddenly, there is a plot twist. The bowl is no longer full, housing the black jelly beans no one wants. They have disappeared. You will find a variety of colored jelly beans and barely a black one in sight.

Yes, the black jelly bean has grown up and people have, too!

As the advocate for the beautiful, black jelly-bean, I stand firm in my commitment to and for HER! The acquired taste is now desired by many. No longer will she languish in bowls that do not value her presence. The delicacy of her consumption has the other BEANS striking poses, wishing they could be as revered. Are you with her? Think about it. Can you relate? Stand up and shout,

"YES, I AM THE BLACK JELLY BEAN!"

All Caught Up

<<<<<<<<<<<<<<<<<<<<<<<<<<<<<<<<<<<<<<<<<<<>

Pitching pennies, wrapping coins
Save, save, save.
Copper, silver, dollar bills
Bank statements, receipts
Watch the balance decrease
Moving ahead from behind
the eight ball
Striving for debt-free status
Once and for all
All caught up is my goal
A Final Payment!

Written/published 2007
The International Who's Who in Poetry, Page 1
The International Library of Poetry; Howard Ely, Editor

Dear Friend

◇◇◇

I thank you for preparing this man for a meaningful relationship. I thank you for sharing him with me. Life lessons learned through communication both past and present add to his perception of true love and passion.

I thank you for bringing out his genuine qualities: responsibility, respect, trustworthiness, wit, emotional stability and a genuine heart. You have taught him how to live and love.

For this, I am thankful. Through him, to know you is to love you – even in death. You are ever-present in thought because you are not forgotten. Thank you for understanding that he deserved to be happy, and for sending him to me.

Sister, Sister

◇◇◇

You are my very first friend and our encounters never end. We know and understand each other's feelings and we know each other's hurts. Neither of us wants to see any situation fail so we support each other through all the ups and downs; we cry together, laugh together; we talk and expose our vulnerabilities that reveal our truths.

Sister, Sister!

I will always be there for you. I will never let you down. Despite our disagreements, drama, and cattiness; ultimately, we come together and acknowledge our loyalty to and for each other. I love you and you love me; our friendship will forever be. When you need me, I'm there!

We should never forget the times past where we had such fun! Although those days are gone, they remain in the forefront of my mind. You have been true and kind to me and I love my Sister!

When

When will I know that love really exists?
When will I know that time hasn't been wasted?
When will I know two people who really care can share?
When will a bond be cherished forevermore?
When. How and why do people lose sight for their
    path seems bright.
Is it wise to know?
It's so confusing
Is it worth investing time?
Do I really want this?
The decision is mine, but I must follow my heart
I'm crying aloud, "Please guide me correctly!"

Leave Me Alone

<><><><><><><><><><><><><><><><><><><><><><><><><><>

It's over and done and the heartaches have been pushed aside. You can no longer cling to me like those dirty old jeans you felt were more important. I have moved on and started anew. I can't be your post to lean on. If you could see me now, you would squirm in your shoes.

Happiness, respect, honesty, and trust were the intent. These things were more than you could give – not what you wanted. Or perhaps, you didn't know how to respond in kind. I am at peace with the many decisions I've made. I have a strong sense of self and I am beautiful!

I Am Not Alone

◇◇

I am not alone
I am not alone
I finally realized, I'm not alone
Times were rough and hard
A whirlwind of mayhem and confusion
Frustration sinks in and you just don't know what
    to do.
Suddenly, your eyes open and the reality of life
consumes you.
Family, friends, and the one who holds a special place
    in your heart confirm your joy.
You stand and shout, "I am not Alone!"

My Gentleman,
My Friend

◇◇◇

Everything happens for a reason, and I want you to know that you are very special and I am truly grateful to have a friend like you in my life. I feel so comfortable around you and so at ease. Each day and each conversation with you has been rewarding and mentally challenging. I sit in my room, at work, and in the car thinking about how relaxed you make me feel despite the drama going on around me. You have expressed to me that the things I will encounter from now on won't be easy, but I will get through them. This is the year of "I will" and I believe the positive vibes I get from supportive, positive people like yourself is all that is needed to confirm my true feelings.

You are a source of inspiration for a lot of people. They look to you for advice, support, a listening ear, and you can provide comfort just by being you. One never knows what people truly think of them until it is too late, and they never get the chance to express their feelings. I am a positive individual who is confident and has a strong sense of self. You have helped me look at a lot of things differently and I was able to do so without clouded judgment. It is different, and I like it!

Someone to talk to

Someone to laugh with

Someone to share with

Someone who for a change is REAL!

I can only speak for myself. I am your friend and I truly hope you are mine. I have experienced some feelings that have overwhelmed me, and they are triggered by my association with you. I know that others probably have the same feelings. You don't need to change. You are a very mild-mannered, respectable, and gentle man. I know this is going to be a good year for you as for me; with a friend like you there is no way I can lose my confidence to continue to strive for the best.

Gaze

◇◇◇

When I look into your eyes, I see your soul; I seek your inner space that makes you tick. You never leave me wondering but my nerve endings make me shed the skin I'm in. I'm naked standing before you free. The tremble of my thighs, prepare for the excitement of the gift that awaits you. Our movement is like poetry in motion; can you feel the juices flowing?

Love in the Air

Love in the air
So fresh, so new
Love in the air
A love that is true
Two lives intertwined
Unknown to each other
Searching for that special one
Who would change your path?
Unity
For you were meant to be
Together as a pair
Displaying "Love in the Air"

New Meaning, New Love

<><><><><><><><><><><><><><><><><><><><><><><><><>

We came together because of a new millennium. Knowing and visualizing beautiful encounters filled with energy, trust, romance, and openness are not new to us. We must believe in each other and never let others define us. The accomplishments we make together will be even greater than those in the past. The depth of our friendship teaches us that we are strong, stable, and confident about how we will continue to contribute to the growth of our love.

A woman must wonder how she could be so lucky to find a man like you! Others before me had no vision or foresight to even trust the test of time. Well, I have found the emotional link and tie that binds us together and it will continue to flourish. I never looked back when you arrived, and I plan to move forward with you.

I Ate Too Much

◇◇◇

When I'm nauseated, I don't feel like myself? My body is on edge and my stomach at full capacity. Overeating creates this uncomfortable state. I must watch my portions. My consumption is not what it used to be.

Here I was thinking I could hang and just eat a little more than usual and I was wrong. I've just made myself miserable and I can't sleep. Hopefully, this will pass and the food I ate will digest. I wish I could regurgitate but the thought of it makes me feel worse. I took one for the TEAM!

My Pain

◇◇

My pain is bearable; but it sometimes becomes intense. My pain attempts to keep me bound knowing I never let grass grow under my feet. My pain strikes at the most inconvenient times as a way of interrupting any plans I may have. I do my best to connect with my pain because it tries me mentally.

When I'm in sync with my pain, I can ease the severity with my will for comfort. Understanding your body and how pain affects it allows you to realize that you have the power to control your pain without it controlling you. My pain doesn't thrive alone; if it doesn't have me, it doesn't exist!

Chocolate Love

◇◇◇

Chocolate Love from above,
Were you sent to me to spend
your destiny?
Spinning and twisting like a top
as our hearts pirouette like a ballerina on stage.
We dance to the beat of love
While holding you tight, I smell a pear and I
bite you to taste your nectar.
As your juices begin to flow across my lips,
I close my eyes to the melodic sound of soft moans.
Hands running through my hair while your fingers
caress my ear signaling to me, it is time.
Your body trembles ever so gently,
your mouth releases sweet gasps of breath into the air
as the room begins to fill with
"Chocolate Love."

My Special Valentine

◇◇

You have the charm that puts the squeeze on an unsuspecting and innocent woman. It's the kind of feeling that makes one yearn for more! As the days go by, you get closer and closer to my heart in a way that no one has ever done.

You are a gem! The man that every woman wants in her life because you represent confidence, ambition, sacrifice, commitment, and romance. It's nice to know that all of these things can be found in one place – You!

On this Valentine's Day, may all the treasures you have stored be revealed.

Forever Yours!

Happy Valentine's Day!

Written/Published 2000

Playmate

You are a fun-loving man who enjoys having a good time. There is an abundance of love in your heart that you share in your own special way. Obstacles are sometimes in our midst, and they require a great deal of concern, but you persevere not allowing anyone or anything to distract your concentration. Self-determination, charisma, and wit are a few qualities that describe you, but they don't express the depth of your genuine soul. You've got it going on so keep your head up because it gets better with time.

We Are One

<><><><><><><><><><><><><><><><><><><><><><><><><><><><><><>

I saw you standing at the altar as I began my walk
    towards you. You were strong, confident, and
    ready to receive me!
As I got closer, reality set in. I was certain that we
    would be joined in holy matrimony and true to
    each other for the rest of our lives.
We are one! We are one!
Best friends, lovers and soul mates –
What a combination! The sparkle in your eye, your
    gentle touch, and respect you display is awe-
    some! It is evident and shows throughout your
    daily activities. Don't you know, baby,
I'm yours because "We Are One!"

Spicy Sorors of SO

◇◇◇◇◇◇◇◇◇◇◇◇◇◇◇◇◇◇◇◇◇◇◇◇◇◇◇◇◇◇◇◇◇◇◇◇

Hey, Soror, what's your name? They call me Elektra and the sister circle fellowship is my claim to fame. When you're seasoned, that "It" factor hits a different way because a ninth spice was revealed today.

Spicy, spicy, love them so;

Once you're welcomed, you never let go. I'm here to tell you they love their pink and green and when you see one, it's like living a dream. My sister, my sister, our love will forever grow. The Spicy Sorors of South Orange are ageless beauties on the go!

Not Sorry, for the Sorry

◇◇◇◇◇◇◇◇◇◇◇◇◇◇◇◇◇◇◇◇◇◇◇◇◇◇◇◇◇◇◇◇◇◇◇◇◇◇◇

I'm not sorry for you. You can never tell the truth. You don't know the truth. Lies, Lies and more lies! How can you be any good or help to another? You rely on the strength of anyone who calls themselves your brother.

I'm not sorry for you. You don't take responsibility for what you do. You pull the wool over the eyes of unsuspecting women: who only know what you tell them. How can you live these lies? You don't file taxes; You don't take care of your children, and you expect people to do for you. What do you do for them?

I'm not sorry for you. You are like an anchor weighing a person down. You cheat and scheme to get over. You do have a past. You cannot erase it until you confront it with your eyes wide open. No one will ever KNOW YOU. You will never have anything.

I'm not sorry for you. You can't start over, for the past will catch you. All of your lies will be known one day. I don't have to tell it! Because You Live It! They will All see what You came to be – A whole lot of nothing! Hiding behind anything good will be your legacy – The Lack of Truth! I hope no one else gets hurt in your midst, for your demise will begin swiftly! I'm not sorry, for the Sorry.

Mommy's Baby Girl

◇◇◇◇◇◇◇◇◇◇◇◇◇◇◇◇◇◇◇◇◇◇◇◇◇◇◇◇◇◇◇◇◇◇◇◇◇◇◇

Time is moving by swiftly and you are growing up fast. Decisions are crucial and time is of the essence. You are about to begin the start of a new chapter in your life called "Adulthood." No longer will you have to take direction but instead, you will determine your direction.

You are Mommy's baby girl, and I love you so much. It's hard to say goodbye to the memorable moments we've shared during your childhood. "Moving on up," is what they call it. Do not forget the life skills you were taught; be strong so you can conquer the world. "I believe in you!"

Ripper

<><><><><><><><><><><><><><><><><><><><><><><><><>

It's a tasked responsibility being the master of all trades. Running around making sure the children and friends get to and from their individual destinations becomes daunting to say the least, but we do it anyway.

The commitment to living a full life is overrated as the Pearl makes her way through everything thrown at her. Why are we so resilient? Why do we nurture with such queenlike posture?

Is there a match to this kind of reign? One thing is for sure, a mother's love is one of a kind that surpasses all. She's a RIPPER!

Expression of Love

<><><><><><><><><><><><><><><><><><><><><><><><><><><><>

What makes me adore you? Is it the way you smile or the smile upon my face when I see you or just the thought of you?

It's simple. You keep the laughter alive and present thought-provoking challenges that contribute to our natural vibe.

Why do I adore you? The electricity between us is part of a grid that screams "We got this!" It's a soul-deep connection that attracts and captivates the two of us.

It's easy. You bring the sunshine on a dark, gloomy day that's never-ending, spewing expressions of love!

So Long

◇◇◇◇◇◇◇◇◇◇◇◇◇◇◇◇◇◇◇◇◇◇◇◇◇◇◇◇◇◇◇◇◇◇◇◇◇

I must say it's been a great ride. I'm not a fan of befriending anyone just for something to do. I opened up to you more than I expected; encountered and tolerated behaviors that I am in no position to question and gave of myself because I like you; was comfortable with you; tried to understand without judgment and wanted you to be free to be yourself when we were together.

Friendship is so important and the foundation of any relationship. I believed you and kept my relationship with you as quiet as I could, understanding I couldn't ask or expect more than you were willing to give.

Thank you for showing me who you are; what you're made of and that people like you can exist but NOT at this time. I'm worth more; deserving of more; want more; and want to give the same in return. I can wait! I'm perplexed but not bound enough to figure it out. I'd rather focus on what's in front of me moving forward. I understand it is, what it ain't, and the likelihood of a tomorrow with you is not in the foreseeable future. I was navigating my "right now" with you. So long!

You Date Well

You date well!
Always thinking of the best and making sure it's an
    experience never to forget
You date well!
Your presentation and effortless ability to expose me
    to things is priceless
You date well!
Knowing what a lady should have and ensuring she
    gets it
You date well!
Keeping the atmosphere light and airy without
    interruption
You certainly date well!
Loving the union with affirmation of how you feel in
    the moment
We date well!
Ending the night with a kiss yearning to see each
    other again to continue growing our
special bond!

Just Believe

I knew it was you
The way our eyes met on top of the star
It was you who made the promise of no-failure belief
    from afar
As the moonlight glistens upon my skin
You clear the way for a perfect landing
Into a chocolate heaven full of goodness where you
    are safe
Many to most encounter an unsubstantiated love.
It matters not the outcome but how they navigate
    the deceit
Never allowing the negativity to infiltrate their core
    but instead focusing on what's true
She assures you never to repeat the days of old – Just
    Believe!

Transformation

◇◇◇

I say yes to transformation: out with the OLD to create a brand new YOU! Establishing and embracing a routine that will enable one to focus on making better life choices in every aspect of life. Think of it as a rebirth. Depending on the circumstances, you get the opportunity to emerge fresh, with new ideas and ways to effectively live life and love on your own terms.

Finding Your Happy

◇◇

Have you ever thought to yourself, am I happy? Do you even know what triggers leave you in that happy space? How do you present your happy?

After careful consideration and reviewing the definition of what happiness is, I have concluded as I'm sure many of you have too, that I love myself enough to know that my complete connection with my inner self (mind, body, & soul) gives me the ability to proclaim my happiness. How so, you ask? I believe in self-care/self-love, stimulating my mind, and accepting my authenticity in all that I do.

I posted on Facebook a quote that said: "Psychologists say, once you learn how to BE HAPPY you won't tolerate being around people who make you feel anything less!"

Satisfaction with different areas of your life makes a huge difference when you take inventory of the things you've done and what you consider important. Happiness is an emotional state that YOU create as a result of your decisions (work, relationships, hobbies, etc.).

No one dictates your happy or happiness. If they're important enough to be in your life, they would be an added attraction and more like a cherry on top of what you already know and feel.

Understanding your happiness is a personal endeavor. Joy and contentment contribute to your life satisfaction. Sitting in a quiet place, reviewing the pros/cons of things that affect your life, thinking/living healthy, and choosing You over everything else will give you a sense of happy even if you didn't realize it.

My Knight

◇◇◇◇◇◇◇◇◇◇◇◇◇◇◇◇◇◇◇◇◇◇◇◇◇◇◇◇◇◇◇◇◇◇

You came in strong, swept me and captured my heart. You showed me what my father ALWAYS said should happen when a man asks for your hand. YOU DID THAT!

I was your QUEEN before you ever told me and now you're my KING! The way you hold me and profess your love is more than one could ask for. Your attentiveness to detail and knowing what to do or say at any given moment confirms how special you are and have been in my life.

The intuition is addictive and when two minds come together as we have, there's nothing better than a great escape. You are a planner, ready to go and as you say, "let's make it happen." Well, it's happening!

We deserve everything that awaits us; navigating our spaces has been a pleasure and although I'm admittedly biased, our feelings are a force field of progressive energy. You are a constant supporter of everything I do; you never waiver and you ensure I always have the best.

Here's to you, my King; my confidante; my lover; my friend – you know who you are!

Until we meet…

We Are in This Together

What a blessing it is to be amongst the living today! We are ALL human and have made mistakes, but they are not mistakes that cannot be corrected. I refuse to allow You to be stuck in a place where you feel the road to success we're on doesn't come without construction work. We are all successful and those of us who want something more will fight through both the highs and the lows to get where we need to be. Let's finish what we started STRONG! We determine how this mission is implemented! We dictate how swift we move through this endeavor. We are crucial to the blessings bestowed upon others and those that come to us. We're going to kill the lost, abandoned, confused, I don't know what to do positions, and restart ourselves. Supporting one another as opposed to sitting back, watching and waiting for someone else's errors/faults makes you part of the problem.

Well, I'm here to tell you and others today that none of us are problems! We are solution-driven and will emerge victorious when we forge ahead with the mindset we had when we joined this group. We don't cheat each other. We lift each other up so that every day is better than yesterday as a family!

Let's do this and make TODAY and the days to come bring a smile to faces near and far!

My Greeting

◇◇◇

Most Gracious Lady Romy

You are the Leader of all things that are Gracious and Fine.

You, Goddess Elektra, are the STAR that always shines.

Your movements inspire a tune and a dance.

Your grandiose presence puts others in a trance. It is in you, we see an definable magnificence.

Speaker of the Word,

Lover of Divine,

Most Gracious Lady Romy,

"You are One of a Kind!"

Crack Repair

<><><><><><><><><><><><><><><><><><><><><><><><><><><><>

I find myself amused in the wee hours of the morning thinking about the crack repair that needs to take place in my life. It matters not how strong I think I am because somehow, someway, cracks appear. I don't know the cause, but it certainly creates moments of pause in my routine.

My sturdy foundation has encountered a stir that needs more than an adjustment. I found the weak link and I must nurture and make it whole again. Filling the crack involves understanding myself and recognizing I am not as flawless as I'd like to be. The crack repair teaches me a lesson about maintenance and the importance of it in my life. The comeback is better, I'm prepared, and this is no Band-Aid affair!

Family Reunion

<><><><><><><><><><><><><><><><><><><><><><><><><>

Grandma, GP, Mommy, Daddy, Auntie, Uncle,
    Sister, Brother, Niece, Nephew
are the ties that bind us together. The pots are full,
    the pies smell good, table
settings and we give thanks. Prayers and hugs, music
    and fellowship.
Cars. Planes. Buses, trains traveling the roads to one
    destination. Tireless
waiting and loss of sleep awaiting the appointed time
    to meet.

Speak to My Heart

◇◇◇◇◇◇◇◇◇◇◇◇◇◇◇◇◇◇◇◇◇◇◇◇◇◇◇◇◇◇◇◇◇◇

The sleeve was affixed to my arm and with the use of the stethoscope, she listened to my pulse and counted the beats of my heart. Although we were not one, it was as though she could speak to my heart. I could feel the pulse that grew louder and faster. It was like inside chatter that had its own agenda. Never had I thought to listen other than when at the doctor.

The anxiety of receiving results aligns your thoughts as you pray for a good report. Bodies close enough to mirror movement allow you to feel my heart, listen to my heart and speak to my heart. We've got something special here: "I'm open, are you?"

No One to Blame

<><><><><><><><><><><><><><><><><><><><><><><><><>

There's an array of emotional turmoil that keeps me in a space of uncertainty. It's like being amid an internal fog. I try to rationalize and figure out how to convince myself what I'm doing is right. All the while, I cannot identify the "WHY" of my actions.

Tears flow down my cheek escaping the unknown. My blood pressure elevates while my heart beats like it's running a race. How do I make sense of this? I thought I had tough skin and what I really had was hurt feelings.

We Need Prayer

◇◇◇◇◇◇◇◇◇◇◇◇◇◇◇◇◇◇◇◇◇◇◇◇◇◇◇◇◇◇◇◇◇◇◇◇◇◇

Dear Lord, I am feeling uneasy, and I know this is Not a space you would have me in. I'm asking that discernment be scattered amongst this group so that collectively We can resolve whatever has gone awry. You know my life and more importantly, you know my heart. You know that without detail, I specifically move with purpose. I find delight in the success of others; and I am not quick to judge.

Communication is key to me, and currently, the lack of it is a contributing factor of My uneasiness. I call on you daily and I listen because sometimes I find myself having to guard my tongue. This is one of those times. Clarity about a host of things is very Cloudy right now and I'm praying for understanding for All who read and hear this prayer. Until I receive a call, this is All I have. Amen.

A Wedding Prayer

◇◇

Although life changes happen all the time, I don't think you're ever ready to look at life through the eyes of your child. You know the day comes when they make life choices and decisions on their own and this Is what parents pray for.

May today and everyday be inspiring, loving, and full of happiness. As you embark on the beginning of a new union and most important part of your life, I want you to know that you are blessed and loved! I am so proud of you and pray that today and every day to come are creatively crafted by the two of you.

Loving you both today and always,

Mackin'

◇◇

I'm a serious, Mack.

Been married twice so you can't come for me without
any money.

Everything Costs!

I need gifts.

Do you paint? Do you have any skills at all!

You don't get access to all my goodies when you're
empty-handed.

Step your game up and holla back when you're
straight.

I'm making moves and I'm not taking anyone along
for the ride.

There's no time for feelings.

They don't live here anymore.

My Best Friend

◇◇◇

Hmmmm…

I love the idea of marriage but with a man who will love all of me. I know how to love a man unconditionally and that has Never been an Achilles' heel for me. I've made some decisions that forced me to grow up alone while in a relationship. I believed the relationship growth would be a joint venture, but I was wrong. People bring their own baggage to a situation without disclosing what it is they truly want. I didn't do that and found that it didn't matter how much I knew or didn't know about my mate, they had different agendas based on what I could do for them as opposed to a united front comprised of the two of us.

I know there's no "I" in team but the "I" only worked when I was alone. I don't consider my being single a "newfound freedom" but from the onset, it was an impending reality. I continued to look at the snapshot of my life and really started to love me more than ever. I saw Me and saw how my nonconforming behavior made those I was aligned with irritated to the point they didn't like me; they competed against me; they belittled me; they tried to knock me down a few pedestals and tried to defame me.

I am a Warrior! I may wipe a little dust off, but I am never knocked down nor will I ever be. I am resilient and I love hard. I AM a nurturer, and I don't want to be anyone else's mother. I want to be a "Pahtna." I've relaxed a lot and I've allowed myself to experience things and people differently. I'm a learner and I'm not going to stand in my own way by closing anything off.

I know I'm an intimate being. I also know that I have not been in a relationship where intimacy has developed and blossomed. I could express a number of sexual expectations, but I don't. I am not in the space where I need physical sex daily, weekly, or monthly. Don't get me wrong because it's most definitely enjoyable but only with the one you want to be with. I am sapiosexual and many to most men can't handle it because they don't identify. I gravitate to you daily because you are strong in your spot, and I am satisfied without physically touching. It is sexy as hell, and it creates a desired crave.

Will I ever get married again? I hope so, but what I can say is that I'm not wasting any more time with people who haven't mapped out any plans for themselves. I want to be led and I want to be supportive, but I also want those things reciprocated. My dream is to one day know in my heart that my man is proud of me beyond measure and can stand firmly and say, "There goes my baby!" I want my love to be so apparent that others will be in awe of how much affection we openly share. I know it is real and can be achieved. I also know that all the pieces that involve loving someone and liking them too represents my best friend!

Life Shows Up

<><><><><><><><><><><><><><><><><><><><><><><><><>

As we go about our daily routine, we don't do a great job telling our youth that life shows up. When there's a loss of a loved one, you've got to adjust. You don't have to do it alone. Life will keep showing up even when sickness occurs, and you do not have the antibodies to fight it!

When in the lowest of lows in your life, you must figure out your new normal. Turning your back on a loved one in a time of need is considered an unfavorable act and walking away is never easy. Risks and Costs: There is a difference!

You have options. We all grieve differently. Why do we always have to be the one to always stick it out. There's a famine in the land taking people out and everyone has drama all around them. I took my out!

Pep Talk: I summoned my strength in order to take control of myself and make a final decision. I rested and remembered where I came from by returning to the place I was nurtured. It doesn't mean I was starting over but I needed to be cared for.

To stay when I needed to leave was a betrayal to myself. It is well! I chose myself. It is well with my soul. There's nothing wrong with choosing You! Wanting to be loved and needing your community; being in solitude with God; relearning how to reset and knowing God will be with you every step of the way.

There's nothing wrong with giving a benediction. You must give a benediction and send people forth in love. I love you and still I must do this to get my healing to find out what God has in store for me while still leaving the door open for return.

A Love Gained, A Love Free

<><><><><><><><><><><><><><><><><><><><><><><><><><><><><>

He valued Family with every fiber of his being. He showered me and our daughters with an embracing love to be proud of and to emulate. Although outnumbered at home, he led the way providing guidance and instruction in a manner that garnered respect and admiration.

There's something to be said for a man who was able to live a fully engaged life despite battling health challenges seen and unseen. He kept the faith, prayed, and kept moving. The five of us had an amazing, fun-filled life. There was never a time that our home was not filled with laughter, and it was remarkable! Everything we did together was a teaching moment for our daughters and whatever it was always ended with one of his infamous lectures. He earned the hashtag "Girl Dad" before it ever became a trending topic.

He was a blessing to me. It matters not what we encountered in twenty years because we remained besties. I loved him and I knew he loved me! I'm going to miss speaking to him daily and talking about our daughters, our grandson AND participating in his financial freedom seminars with an audience of one – ME!

Rest in Paradise! I never knew a kinder man. Even if we were miles apart, I will forever be his lady and he was my gent. He was my Love! A loved gained, A love free!

Love Don't Live Here Anymore

◇◇◇◇◇◇◇◇◇◇◇◇◇◇◇◇◇◇◇◇◇◇◇◇◇◇◇◇◇◇◇◇◇◇◇◇◇◇

We used to go places and do a lot of things before we had children. Once the babies arrived, there was a new game going on and I wasn't in it. I learned quite a few life lessons – I am an excellent student and a good study. My feelings, emotions, and outlook on life as I knew it were long gone. The difference is that I was all alone on this quest striving to have the perfect life and family. When the love is gone, nothing else can survive. Everyone feels it. Your demeanor affects everyone and everything you touch.

It is sad when the inevitable is staring you in the face and you don't know or see it. I was so over my example, and he couldn't man up and acknowledge it. Everything comes with a price tag. You get nothing for free. I once told him, he has dreams; but he never sees what he hopes to achieve through to fruition. We had thoughts and dreams as a couple, but you know, I guess I was the only one who really cared.

My divorce was quite simple because there weren't many details. It did, however, take one year, ten months, and two days to become final – "Judgment By default." Love don't live here anymore!

Unwavering

◇◇◇

A clear unwavering of self will work tirelessly for you. Compassion and empathy for those defined by my sense of loyalty no matter the obstacles put in my way.

My job is not over. There is more for me to offer and do. A passion to assist in cultivating and developing young minds as they discover and identify their talents.

A Birthday Tribute to Me

◇◇◇

As I reflect on the past fifty-seven years (really thirty with twenty-seven years of experience), I have embraced my formative years as a very mild dysfunctional form of what children today experience. I encountered all kinds of craziness from family and friends. I have been an authentic friend to others as well as my own friend. "I AM ME!"

Surviving the perils of high school and college allowed me to be true to myself with a conviction of who I am. This outlasted all the things I questioned about myself and others during my youth. I have lived and learned from many. I've been married, divorced, had three (3) children; I'm a grandmother of two (2), retired, and "I AM STILL ME!"

My education took a hiatus until I consciously revived my desire to be the ME I knew I was by completing two (2) advanced degrees. I have been focusing on ME and doing the things that make ME happy. I have six (6) courses left in the Chronicles of Being Dr. Romy – "THIS IS ME!"

We follow each other's lives and delight mutually in ALL the proud moments, successes, and having support is comforting.

To All my FBF & Family, thank you for your support, well wishes (good and bad) because without them, my navigation through this life would've left me looking unhinged – NEVER! "I AM A BETTER ME!"

I can unapologetically say with certainty that I am proud to be the person I am today standing in strength mixed with fire, pink and green love, and an explosiveness that turns heads including my own, "I SLAY ME!"

On this second day of 2022, My BIRTHDAY, I look forward to celebrating and sharing with you all the BLESSINGS this NEW YEAR will bring us and I might add that "We do need them!"

"I AM ME; YOU ARE YOU & WE ARE WE!"

Be Aware

◇◇◇◇◇◇◇◇◇◇◇◇◇◇◇◇◇◇◇◇◇◇◇◇◇◇◇◇◇◇◇◇◇◇◇◇◇

And suddenly everything came to a complete Stop!

She was very tired and couldn't speak! No sound at all. She had to rely on hand signals and specific gestures to communicate. She was achy but somewhat fatigued. Feverish on occasion but able to get out of bed to relieve herself. What in the world is everyone going to do as a result of her silence? It's unheard of and something that's never been experienced before.

This is a situation many find themselves in because they don't prepare themselves for the "what will happen when I'm not here" moment. It's Never intentional and you cannot predict it.

Get your lives, people! Life doesn't make or affirm any promises. Until you live in complete silence, you won't understand. This is my current situation. If you need to speak to me, I suggest using FaceTime, text messages, visiting, or writing me a letter. My speaking has been shut down until further notice!

Carry On…

Embracing My Treasure

<><><><><><><><><><><><><><><><><><><><><><><><><><>

I took inventory of my goals and accomplishments. I wanted to document what I've been doing throughout my life and memorialize it on paper. Things look different when you are reading as opposed to someone telling you about themselves.

I have done some incredible things. I never discussed what I've done so it comes as a surprise to some, and others had/have no idea. Learning how to embrace your treasure is not difficult when you allow yourself to flourish. The little things are the detailed specific attributes that magnify your result.

Practice self-love and reward yourself for attaining successes. Enjoy the moment when what you have done helps someone or if they tell you. Let the praise about your great deed speak for you, and your treasures will become insurmountable. If you can do these simple things, you will understand the meaning of embracing your treasure.

About the Author

◇◇

Romy E. Florence is a New Jersey Native whose passion to help others has manifested through picking up the pieces of her life and embracing her treasure. Investing in herself is a promise made, and everything she engages is fulfilled with the richness of love taught and learned from her family.

Retired from law enforcement, a mother of three adult daughters and two grandsons, she humbly lives the life of the Black Swan with grace.

CPSIA information can be obtained
at www.ICGtesting.com
Printed in the USA
BVHW051124031122
651062BV00002B/107

9 781662 484728